The 1980s
Britain in Pictures

The 1980s
Britain in Pictures

PA Photos

AMMONITE
PRESS

First Published 2008 by
Ammonite Press
an imprint of AE Publications Ltd,
166 High Street, Lewes, East Sussex BN7 1XU

Text copyright Ammonite Press
Images copyright PA Photos
Copyright in the work Ammonite Press

ISBN 978-1-906672-14-0

British Cataloguing in Publication Data. A catalogue
record of this book is available from the British Library.

Editor: Paul Richardson
Picture research: PA Photos
Design: Gravemaker + Scott

Colour reproduction by GMC Reprographics
Printed by Colorprint, China

Page 2: Punks for peace. A group of Youth Campaign for Nuclear Disarmament marchers in London for the Rock the Bomb Festival of Peace at Brixton.
7th May, 1983

Page 5: The Prince and Princess of Wales with their son Prince William, a few days before his second birthday, in the garden of Kensington Palace, London. The Princess is expecting her second child in September.
12th June, 1984

Page 6: PM Margaret Thatcher stands in the shell of London's defunct Battersea Power Station, when she renamed the site 'The Battersea'. The famous London landmark was to be converted into a leisure complex, the first of many failed redevelopment plans by successive owners.
8th June, 1988

Introduction

The archives of PA Photos yield a unique insight into Britain's recent past. Thanks to the science of photography we can view the 20th Century more accurately than any that came before, but it is thanks to news photography, and in particular the great news agency that is The Press Association, that we are able now to witness the events that made up life in Britain, not so long ago.

It is easy, looking back, to imagine a past neatly partitioned into clearly defined periods and dominated by landmarks: wars, political upheaval and economic trends. But the archive tells a different story: alongside the major events that constitute formal history are found the smaller things that had equal – if not greater – significance for ordinary people at the time. And while the photographers were working for that moment's news rather than posterity, the camera is an undiscriminating eye that records everything in its view: to modern eyes it is often the backgrounds of these pictures, not their intended subjects, that provide the greatest fascination. Likewise we see that Britain does not pass neatly from one period to another.

If ever a decade formed a bridge between the past and the future it was the 1980s, and the twin pillars of this bridge were money and technology. Who, in 1979, would have imagined that a portable telephone would become both a fashion item and an essential, not just for business people but for schoolchildren too? Who could have predicted that a career in finance might be glamorous and exciting? At the beginning of the decade personal computers, mobile telephones, credit cards, share ownership and property speculation didn't feature highly in the lives of ordinary people, but by its end they seemed to dominate it.

While these tectonic plates were quietly shifting there was much to see in the news: conflict in the Falklands, Brixton, Northern Ireland and on the picket lines of the steel and coal industries; bombs in London, Brighton and in the air above Lockerbie – it would be easy to see the decade in those terms alone. But this was also the era of Live Aid and the Children in Need appeal, when celebrities began to exploit the media's new satellite and telecommunication powers for altruistic good, the public responding with an overwhelming and unprecedented generosity.

Money and technology, changing Britain both above and below the surface.

England's Bryan Robson (R) volleys the ball past Ireland's Tony Grealish (L) in the European Championship Qualifier – England v Ireland at Wembley Stadium.
6th February, 1980

Pop artist Andy Warhol (C), best known for his giant Campbell's soup pictures, at the Arts Council Shop in London where he was signing copies of his book.
8th February, 1980

The England rugby union team who are marching toward the Triple Crown and the Grand Slam after victories over Ireland, France and Wales. Back row (L-R): Dusty Hare, Phil Blakeway, Paul Dodge, Roger Uttley, Maurice Colclough, John Scott, Fran Cotton, Clive Woodward, Tony Neary and Peter Wheeler. Front row (L-R): John Horton, Mike Slemen, Billy Beaumont (captain), Steve Smith, John Carleton, Alan Old and G Peck.
18th February, 1980

Police officers eat lunch,
as they take a break
from coping with a mass
picket of the steel works at
Sheerness. The 14-week
strike, which began in BSC
plants but spread to privately
owned steel works such as
Sheerness, was the first in
the steel industry for over 50
years.
20th February, 1980

England's Steve Smith (C) feeds his backs from a maul in the Five Nations Championship – Scotland v England – Murrayfield.
15th March, 1980

The Humber Bridge, the world's longest single span suspension bridge, during its final stages of construction. The decision to build the bridge was taken in 1969, work started in 1972 and it was finally opened in 1981.

21st March, 1980

Anti-nuclear power
demonstration at Trafalgar
Square.
29th March, 1980

Kevin Keegan (L) and Henry
Cooper (R) fool around in
a miniature boxing ring to
promote Brut 33 aftershave.
31st March, 1980

'Superbed', the bed that has
everything. This bed has a
'his' and 'hers' television,
computer controls and a
device to set the mood of
the moment – all for a mere
£80,000.
1st April, 1980

When England received the Rugby Union Team of the Year Trophy, Bill Jnr, a four week old lion cub, was given to captain Bill Beaumont who is also captain of the British Lions.

17th April, 1980

Jake Mangel Wurzel and
his Wurzel-Wagon. Jake, a
former lorry driver, born John
Grey, changed his name by
deed poll when he appointed
himself Huddersfield's
unpaid entertainer.
1st May, 1980

Hooded men (L) on the first floor balcony of the Iranian Embassy in London when two explosions ended the six-day seige at the building in Princes Gate. 14 hostages were brought out alive and a number of gunmen detained.
5th May, 1980

West Ham United fan at
the FA Cup Final against
Arsenal.
10th May, 1980

The Queen, with Corgis, walking the Cross Country course during the second day of the Windsor Horse Trials.

17th May, 1980

Nottingham Forest celebrate
after winning their second
successive European Cup
Final.
28th May, 1980

The Prime Minister, Mrs
Margaret Thatcher, sharing a
joke with England footballers
Kevin Keegan (L), Emlyn
Hughes and other members
of the international squad
outside 10 Downing Street
as they were leaving after
attending a reception.
5th June, 1980

Radio One DJ Kenny
Everett hitting the high notes
outside the BBC TV centre
in London when he joined a
Musicians' Union picket line.
12th June, 1980

The Queen, on her Official Birthday, indicates the direction from which an RAF flypast should come into view for the benefit of three year old Master Peter Phillips and the Earl Of Ulster, who is five. Princess Anne, Master Phillips' mother, stands behind.

14th June, 1980

Trainer Dick Drakes built
a pair of water skis for the
1400 kilo elephant who
appeared in the film 'Honky
Tonk Women'.
30th June, 1980

Great Britain's Daley
Thompson clears the bar
in the high jump in the
Decathlon event at the
Moscow Olympics.
25th July, 1980

New York's Greenwich Village came to St Katherine's Dock in the Pool of London, as the Village People were in the city to launch their movie, 'Can't Stop The Music', after a trip aboard a Thames cruiser.
27th July, 1980

Lady Tavistock and a Tiger Moth outside Woburn Abbey for the celebration of the record-breaking flight of the Duchess of Bedford (Lord Tavistock's grandmother) from England to Cape Town, South Africa, 50 years before.

1st August, 1980

Great Britain's Sebastian Coe (R) wins gold as he crosses the line ahead of East Germany's Jurgen Straub (R, hidden) and teammate Steve Ovett (L) in the Men's 1500m at the Moscow Olympic Games.
1st August, 1980

Prime Minister Margaret Thatcher (third R) hands over a copy of the deeds of 39 Amersham Road, Harold Hill, in Essex, to James Patterson (at front door), the GLC's 12,000th council house buyer. GLC leader Sir Horace Cutler (second R) looks on.

11th August, 1980

Hollywood song and dance star, actor Gene Kelly, sharing his umbrella with new dancing partner Miss Piggy, of 'The Muppet Show', at ATV Studios in Boreham Wood.

19th August, 1980

Actress Barbara Windsor on the Honda 100A, a 100cc commuter bike. She was visiting the International Motor Show at Earls Court in London.
22nd August, 1980

'The lady's not for tickling'.
The Prime Minister,
Mrs Margaret Thatcher,
talking with Ken Dodd at
the London Palladium,
when she attended the
evening performance of the
comedian's 'Laughter Show'.
23rd October, 1980

A youth displays his swastika T-shirt during a British Movement march from Hyde Park to Paddington Recreation Ground. The British Movement is a splinter group of the National Front.

23rd November, 1980

Members of the British Movement hold up a banner with the slogan 'White Power' and give Nazi salutes, during a march from Hyde Park, London, to Paddington Recreation Ground.

23rd November, 1980

As part of her 80th birthday celebration, the Queen Mother visited the Press Club in Shoe Lane, London, where she tried her skill at the snooker table.
3rd December, 1980

Fifteen of radio's best-known disc jockeys eating Christmas Lunch at Broadcasting House: (back row L-R) Simon Bates, Mike Read, Peter Powell, Tommy Vance, Adrian Love and Richard Skinner; (middle row, L-R) Paul Burnett, Andy Peebles, John Peel, Steve Wright, Annie Nightingale, Paul Gambaccini, and Adrian Juste; (front row L-R) Dave Lee Travis and Jimmy Savile.

4th December, 1980

Television personality and dog trainer Barbara Woodhouse with the two winners of the 1980 Pro-Dogs award: Dougal the Pekingese (L), who won the Gold Medal for saving his owner and her daughter from gas fumes, and Kalli (R) who won the Gold Medal for Pet of the Year.
7th December, 1980

The scene outside St George's City Hall in Liverpool, when thousands gathered to pay tribute to the former Beatle after his death by shooting in New York a week earlier.
14th December, 1980

Squatters on a balcony at
Kilver House, a GLC block
of flats at the Oval in South
London, which had been
occupied since the previous
October.
5th January, 1981

Jon Pertwee as Worzel
Gummidge and Una Stubbs
as Aunt Sally, in London for
St Valentines' Day.
4th February, 1981

The Advanced Passenger
Train, British Rail's prototype
tilting train which was later
rejected by the network.
7th February, 1981

Prince Charles and
Lady Diana Spencer at
Buckingham Palace after
the announcement of their
engagement.
24th February, 1981

The Prince of Wales shooting pool in the Pear Tree coffee bar in Derby, a County Council drop-in centre for young people.
27th February, 1981

The England Rugby team got together to raise up this Mini Metro with Union Jack paint-work, whilst training at St Marys College, Teddington, for their match against France.
19th March, 1981

Barry Sheene leading off
the first 20 Royal Mail Radio
Courier Service riders for a
safety 'teach-in' in Battersea
Park.
23rd March, 1981

Milton Keynes Development
Corporation is established
under the New Towns Act
1981.
1st April, 1981

A senior police officer is confronted in Brixton, London, during renewed rioting.
11th April, 1981

Barry Sheene takes a corner during the Transatlantic Trophy at Brands Hatch.
21st April, 1981

Liverpool's winning goalscorer Alan Kennedy celebrates with the European Cup after defeating Real Madrid at the Parc des Princes.
27th May, 1981

'Shergar', Walter Swinburn up, comes home to win the Derby by 15 lengths from 'Glint of Gold', J Matthias up. 'Shergar' was kidnapped two years later by masked gunmen, whose demand for a £2m ransom was refused. The horse was never seen again.

3rd June, 1981

Ian Botham, England, at the Prudential Trophy One Day International, England v Australia.

6th June, 1981

Rod Hull and the aggressive
Emu, famous for attacking
television interviewers such
as Michael Parkinson.
20th June, 1981

Wrestler Giant Haystacks with London postwoman Beverley Calloway, just four feet ten inches tall, at the launch of new British stamps highlighting beauty spots in the care of the National Trust, including the Giants' Causeway (pictured).
23rd June, 1981

A police car blazes at the corner of Atlantic Road and Brixton Road, Brixton, South London in a brief outbreak of violence.
10th July, 1981

Facing page: Fred English of East Molesey stands with pride outside his house decorated for the Royal Wedding of Lady Diana Spencer and Prince Charles. Fred has decorated his house for every Royal event since 1930.
28th June, 1981

Grandmother Kathleen
Lucus, one of many who
made all-night vigils waiting
for the Royal Wedding of
Lady Diana Spencer to
Prince Charles.
28th July, 1981

The newly married Prince
and Princess of Wales
(formerly Lady Diana
Spencer) kiss on the balcony
of Buckingham Palace after
their wedding ceremony at
St. Paul's Cathedral.
29th July, 1981

The Prince and Princess of Wales at Buckingham Palace after their wedding at St Paul's Cathedral.
29th July, 1981

Facing page: The official group photograph at the wedding of the Prince and Princess of Wales.
29th July, 1981

The Queen arrives at London's Heathrow Airport with Corgi puppies, for her flight to Aberdeen and the start of her annual holiday at Balmoral.
5th August, 1981

The Prince and Princess
of Wales pose for
photographers by the banks
of the River Dee during their
Balmoral holiday.
19th August, 1981

Naturalist Desmond Morris
pays a visit to unsuspecting
father-to-be Chia Chia at
Regents Park.
26th August, 1981

Police detain Mod revival Parka-wearing youths in parcel trucks at Brighton station before putting them on the train out of town.
31st August, 1981

(L-R) John Cleese, Rowan Atkinson, David Rappaport (hidden) and Pamela Stephenson, carrying a cardboard cut-out during rehearsals at the Theatre Royal in Drury Lane for the show, 'The Secret Policeman's Other Ball.' The gala is in aid of Amnesty International.

6th September, 1981

Facing page: Princess Anne and her mount 'Stevie B' taking the 20th fence in the Cross Country section of the Burghley Horse Trials at Stamford.

12th September, 1981

Facing page: Lord Lichfield sits on his motorcycle to act as model for six Young Photographers of the Year, after presenting cameras to them as First Prize winners in a national competition.
28th October, 1981

Rubik Cube fever at the Games Day '81 Festival of Indoor Games at the Royal Horticultural Society New Hall, London. The cube proved quite a puzzle for Richard Attwater of the 22nd Wimbledon Cub Scout Group.
26th September, 1981

Sir Harry Secombe with
six young ladies and '3-2-1'
TV game show presenter
Ted Rogers during a River
Thames cruise on the 'MV
Queen Elizabeth', hosted
by Yorkshire TV to launch
their light entertainment
productions for 1982.
29th October, 1981

'For Your Eyes Only' Bond girl Tula at the Supernation Custom Car Show, Olympia. Tula (Caroline Cossey) was later 'outed' as a transsexual by the tabloid press.
30th October, 1981

(L-R) John McEnroe confronts Jimmy Connors at the net during a tempestuous Singles Final in the Benson and Hedges Championships at Wembley.
18th November, 1981

Sales Officer Deborah
Eden with the new range
of telephones which British
Telecom will be selling,
following the opening-up
of the industry to private
companies.
19th November, 1981

The Prince Of Wales
at the Royal College Of
Music, where an honorary
Doctorate in Music was
conferred on him by his
grandmother, the Queen
Mother.
26th November, 1981

Comedian and actor John Inman in Regent Street with the most expensive toy in the world, a £2000 scaled-down petrol driven car from Hamleys, which he uses to drive on stage in the pantomime Mother Goose.

14th December, 1981

Comedian Frankie Howerd
on stage at the London
Coliseum as Prison
Warder Frosch from 'Die
Fledermaus' – the role in
which he makes his debut
with the English National
Opera Company.
30th December, 1981

Jocky Wilson and Bobby George, two of the semi-finalists in the Embassy World Professional Darts championship at Stoke.
15th January, 1982

Rowan Atkinson and Pamela
Stephenson of BBC2's 'Not
the Nine O'Clock News'
on location at Lyndhurst,
Hampshire for their new
series.
25th January, 1982

DJ Dave Lee Travis at the Savoy Hotel, London, where he was voted 'Pipeman of the Year' by tobacco industry workers.
27th January, 1982

Suzi Quatro wearing a pair of 'Second Image' jeans, demonstrating the reason why the company awarded her the title 'Rear of the Year'. Previous winners include Barbara Windsor and Felicity Kendall.
14th February, 1982

Geraldine Rees, on 'Cheers', storms on to the finish after negotiating The Chair. Rees became the first female jockey ever to finish the Grand National.

3rd April, 1982

A Sea Harrier and a Sea
King helicopter together on
the deck of HMS 'Hermes'
as she steams south to the
Falkland Islands.
17th April, 1982

Men aboard HMS 'Hermes' take time out for a little sunbathing on the carrier's flight deck as she heads south with the British naval task force for the Falkland Islands.
18th April, 1982

Four year old Elouise (L)
and six year old Sacha,
at Southampton to wave
goodbye to their Welsh
Guardsman father,
infantryman Jed Philips
(moustache, C) as he leaves
on the requisitioned QE2
with the Falklands task force.
The Welsh Guards suffered
33 fatalities in the conflict.
12th May, 1982

Argentine soldiers captured
at Goose Green are guarded
by a British Royal Marine
as they await transit out of
the area. Goose Green was
captured by men from the
Parachute Regiment.
2nd June, 1982

Argentine soldiers line up to hand in their weapons to Royal Marines just outside Port Stanley on East Falkland, following the Argentine surrender.
17th June, 1982

Facing page: Survivors of the RFA 'Sir Galahad' air attack come ashore in life rafts at San Carlos Bay, as the supply ship blazes in the background.
8th June, 1982

Prince Andrew (later the Duke of York) in the Falkland Islands with a camera. There are still over a hundred uncleared minefields on the islands, 30 British servicemen have died there since the end of the hostilities.

29th June, 1982

Crowds gather to see the first of the company step ashore at Portsmouth from HMS 'Hermes' after she had returned from the South Atlantic, where she was the Falklands Task Force flagship. Prior to the conflict 'Hermes' had been earmarked for scrapping.
1st July, 1982

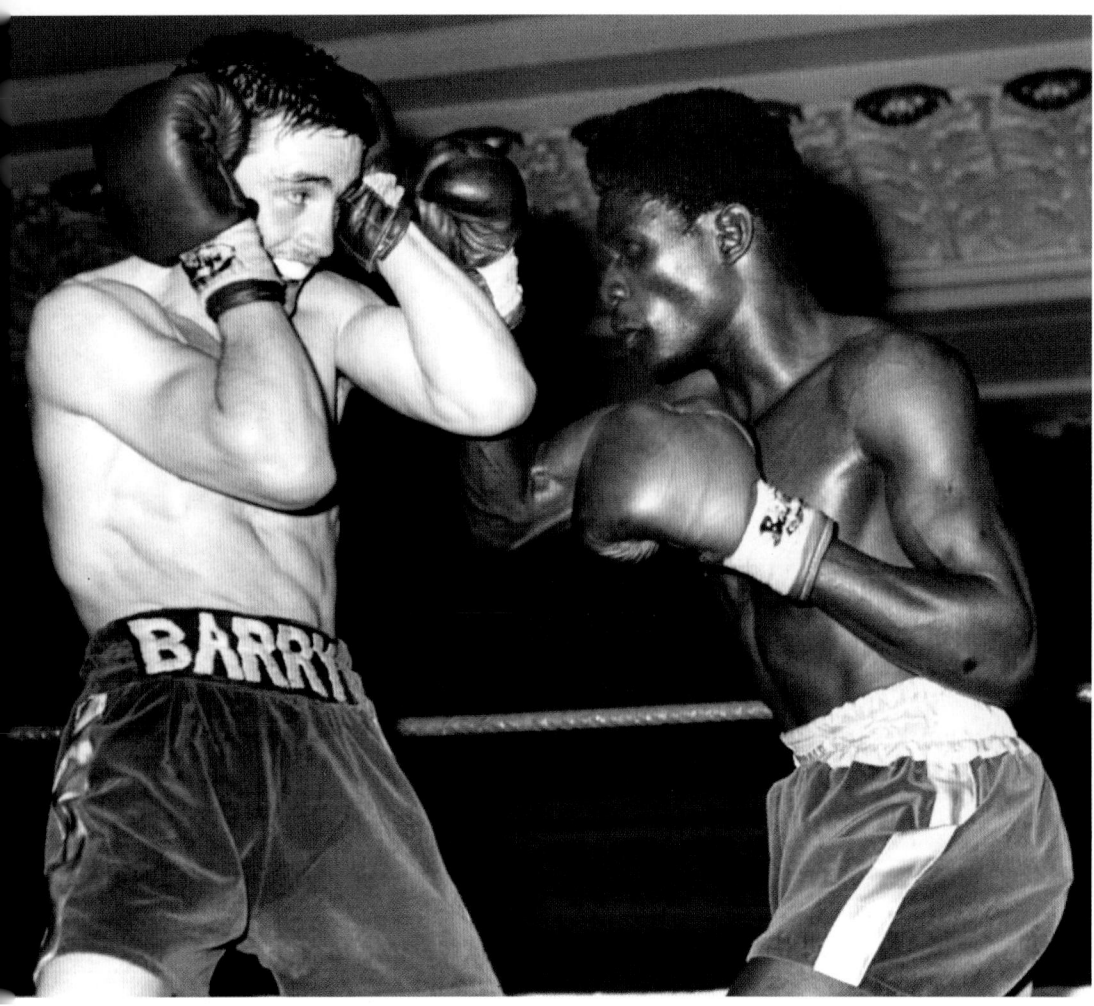

Ireland's Barry McGuigan (L) covers up as Nigeria's Young Ali (real name Asymin Mustapha) attacks. Barry McGuigan would go on to win by knock-out in the sixth round: tragically, Young Ali fell into a coma after the bout and died five months later.
14th June, 1982

England's Paul Mariner enlists the help of a policeman to try to get the ball back from the crowd during the World Cup match against France in Spain.
17th June, 1982

England's Kevin Keegan (L) watches as his header drifts wide of the Spanish goalmouth in the World Cup match.

5th July, 1982

Art Garfunkel (L) and Paul
Simon on stage during
their concert at Wembley
Stadium.
8th July, 1982

Actor Dave Prowse – Darth
Vader in Star Wars – in his
role as the Green Cross
Code Man with youngsters
from Lambeth Johanna
Primary School, London, at
the launch of the London
Accident Prevention
Council's road safety
campaign 'Mind That Child'.
14th July, 1982

Somerset captain Brian
Rose holds the Benson and
Hedges Cup aloft for the
side's supporters to see at
Lord's after their nine wicket
victory over Nottinghamshire
in the final.
24th July, 1982

Swimsuited girls on the
'Cutty Sark' at Greenwich
for the Miss United Kingdom
Beauty Contest. The winner,
who will be the 25th holder
of the title, wins prizes
valued at £15,000 and entry
to the Miss World contest.
22nd August, 1982

Nurses from all over the country parading in London with their protest banners, in support of the TUC's Day of Action on health service pay.

23rd September, 1982

In London, the Birmingham based reggae group Musical Youth, who had a hit with 'Pass the Dutchie'. (foreground to background), Kelvin Grant, 11, Michael Grant, 13, Patrick Waite, 14, Dennis Scaton, 15, Junior Waite, 15.

7th October, 1982

The Queen and Duke of
Edinburgh receive gifts
during their visit to the South
Sea Islands of Tuvalu.
26th October, 1982

The Prince and Princess
of Wales at a ceremony to
name the new Barmouth
Lifeboat, 'The Princess of
Wales'.
25th November, 1982

The Duke of Edinburgh, as
Senior Colonel of the Household
Division, pins the South
Atlantic Medal on Guardsman
Simon Weston, from Gwent,
at Buckingham Palace in
London. Guardsman Weston
was wounded during the attack
on the 'Sir Galahad' in the
Falklands Conflict.
1st December, 1982

An Irish National Liberation
Army bomb killed 11 soldiers
and six civilians at the
Droppin Well disco and bar,
Ballykelly, Northern Ireland.
6th December, 1982

A sit-down protest by women peace campaigners blockading the Greenham Common air base in Berkshire.
13th December, 1982

BBC-TV launched the first breakfast television programme at 6:30 and at the closing stages gathered in the studio for a champagne and cake celebration: (back row L-R) weatherman Francis Wilson, Nick Ross and David Icke; (front row L-R) Jane Pauley, Debbie Rix, Frank Bough (kissing Selina Scott) and astrologer Russell Grant.
17th January, 1983

Marvin Hagler (R) walks into a left from Tony Sibson in their World Middleweight Championship bout. Hagler won in round six.

11th February, 1983

The Prince and Princess of Wales with their baby son, Prince William, at Kensington Palace.
15th March, 1983

Facing page; Sir Richard and Lady Attenborough on arrival at Heathrow Airport, with the Directors' Guild of America Award for the film 'Gandhi'.
14th March, 1983

Nearly twenty years after 'Dr Who' was first broadcast, five incarnations of the BBC TV timelord: (L-R) Richard Hurndall (who plays the late William Hartnell, the first Doctor), Peter Davidson (seated on robot dog K-9), a waxwork model of Tom Baker, John Pertwee, and Patrick Troughton. They are all to feature in a 20th anniversary film 'The Five Doctors'.

17th March, 1983

Delighted Liverpool players (L-R) Graeme Souness, Kenny Dalglish and Alan Hansen celebrate with the Milk Cup trophy after they defeated Manchester United 2-1 in extra time at Wembley.
26th March, 1983

Ventriloquist Keith Harris and his puppet Orville feed a goose in St James's Park, London, to mark the 'Adopt-a-Duck Savings Account', launched jointly by the Wildfowl Trust and the Greenwich Building Society.
12th April, 1983

John Inman camps up the
situation as a new member
joins the cast of 'Are You
Being Served'. Candy Davies
makes her first appearance
in the show being screened
by the BBC.
17th April, 1983

Fashion underwear designer
Janet Reger is back in
business in Knightsbridge,
three months after her
company collapsed with
debts of £1 million.
18th April, 1983

Rock band The Police released their first album for over a year, 'Synchronicity'. They are: (L-R) Sting (Gordon Sumner), Stewart Copeland and Andy Summers. 'Synchronicity' was to be the band's last album.
18th May, 1983

Space Shuttle 'Orbiter Enterprise', mounted on a modified Boeing 747 shuttle carrier aircraft (SCA) during a brief stop for refuelling at RAF Fairford. The Shuttle is on its way to various display points in Europe, including the Paris Air Show.

20th May, 1983

Manchester United's Frank
Stapleton (third R) gets
between Brighton and Hove
Albion's Gary Stevens
(fourth R) and Chris Ramsey
(R) to score the equalising
goal in the FA Cup Final.
21st May, 1983

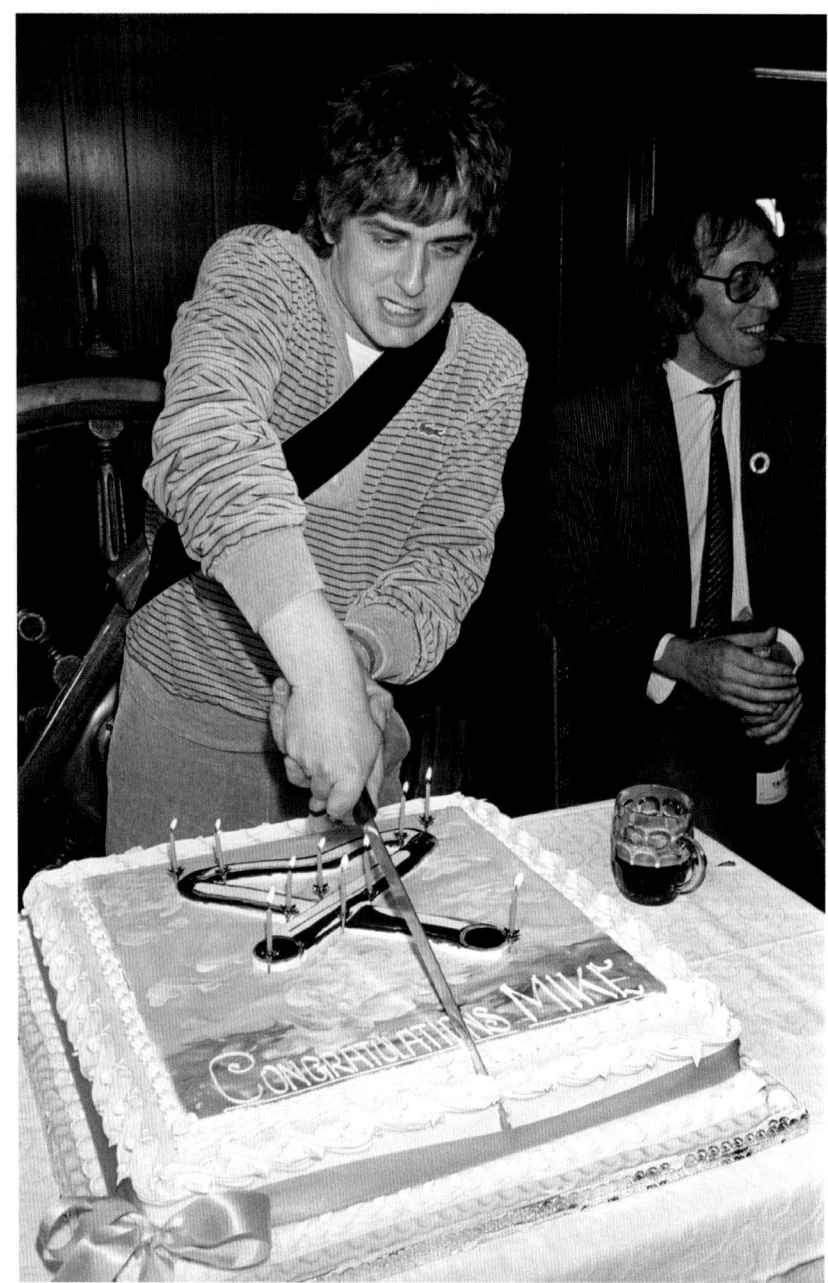

Musician Mike Oldfield cuts a cake to celebrate the 10th anniversary of his album 'Tubular Bells' at a party on a Thames river boat. The cake is decorated to look like the album's cover.
22nd May, 1983

Actor Roger Moore, alias 007 James Bond, in London with seven of the girls who will appear in the new Bond film 'Octopussy': (back row, L-R) Carolyn Seaward, Janine Andrews and Tina Robinson; (front row L-R) Joni Flynn, Alison Worth, Carole Ashby and Mary Stavin.

1st June, 1983

Comedian and DJ Kenny Everett (C) gives Prime Minister Margaret Thatcher a big hand of support, at the Tory Youth Rally at the Wembley Conference Centre. (L-R) Bob Monkhouse, Monty Modlyn, Kenny Everett, Mrs Thatcher, Ted Rogers and Jimmy Tarbuck.

5th June, 1983

Scottish sculptor David Mach in the process of constructing his representation of a Polaris submarine from 5,000 tyres, outside the Hayward Gallery, London.

8th August, 1983

Motorcycle racer Barry
Sheene fools around on a
bicycle with his girlfriend
Stephanie McLean.
15th August, 1983

Steve Cram leads the pack in the Men's 1500m World Championship.
22nd August, 1983

Arsenal fans on the corner of
the North Bank at Highbury,
during a Canon League
Division One game against
Luton Town.
27th August, 1983

Actress Anna Carteret, the
new star of the BBC TV
police series 'Juliet Bravo',
on a bicycle in London.
1st September, 1983

Prince Andrew joins 702
Naval Air Squadron for an
advanced training course on
Lynx helicopters.
19th September, 1983

Undefeated British Heavyweight Frank Bruno (L), weighs in with American opponent Floyd 'Jumbo' Cummings at the London Rooms, before their fight at the Albert Hall.
11th October, 1983

A London bus makes an
unscheduled stop after
reversing into a large hole in
the road.
12th October, 1983

Tottenham Hotspur Football Club's soccer stars (L-R) Garth Crooks, Ossie Ardilles and Danny Thomas stand outside the London Stock Exchange on the club's first day's dealing in its shares.
13th October, 1983

A cascade of champagne down a pyramid of glasses at the British Fashion Ball graced by Princess Michael of Kent at Grosvenor House, London. The Princess drank from the pinnacle glass after she had presented the British Fashion Industry Awards.

13th October, 1983

Neil Kinnock, with his wife Glenys, acknowledges the applause which greeted the announcement of his victory in the Labour Party leadership election in Brighton.
2nd November, 1983

Joan Collins and Leonard Rossiter at the farewell party held at Stringfellows nightclub by Cinzano, to commemorate the last run of the famous adverts in which Collins, as 'Melissa', pours the drink over Rossiter.
18th November, 1983

Facing page: The Queen presents Mother Teresa, winner of the Nobel Peace Prize in 1979, with the insignia of the Honorary Order of Merit.
24th November, 1983

Prince Edward, youngest
son of the Queen and the
Duke of Edinburgh, in a
determined pose during
rehearsals for the Arthur
Miller play 'The Crucible' at
Jesus College, Cambridge.
28th November, 1983

The remains of the Austin 1100 used in the IRA car bomb attack which killed five people outside the Harrods Store in Hans Crescent, London.

18th December, 1983

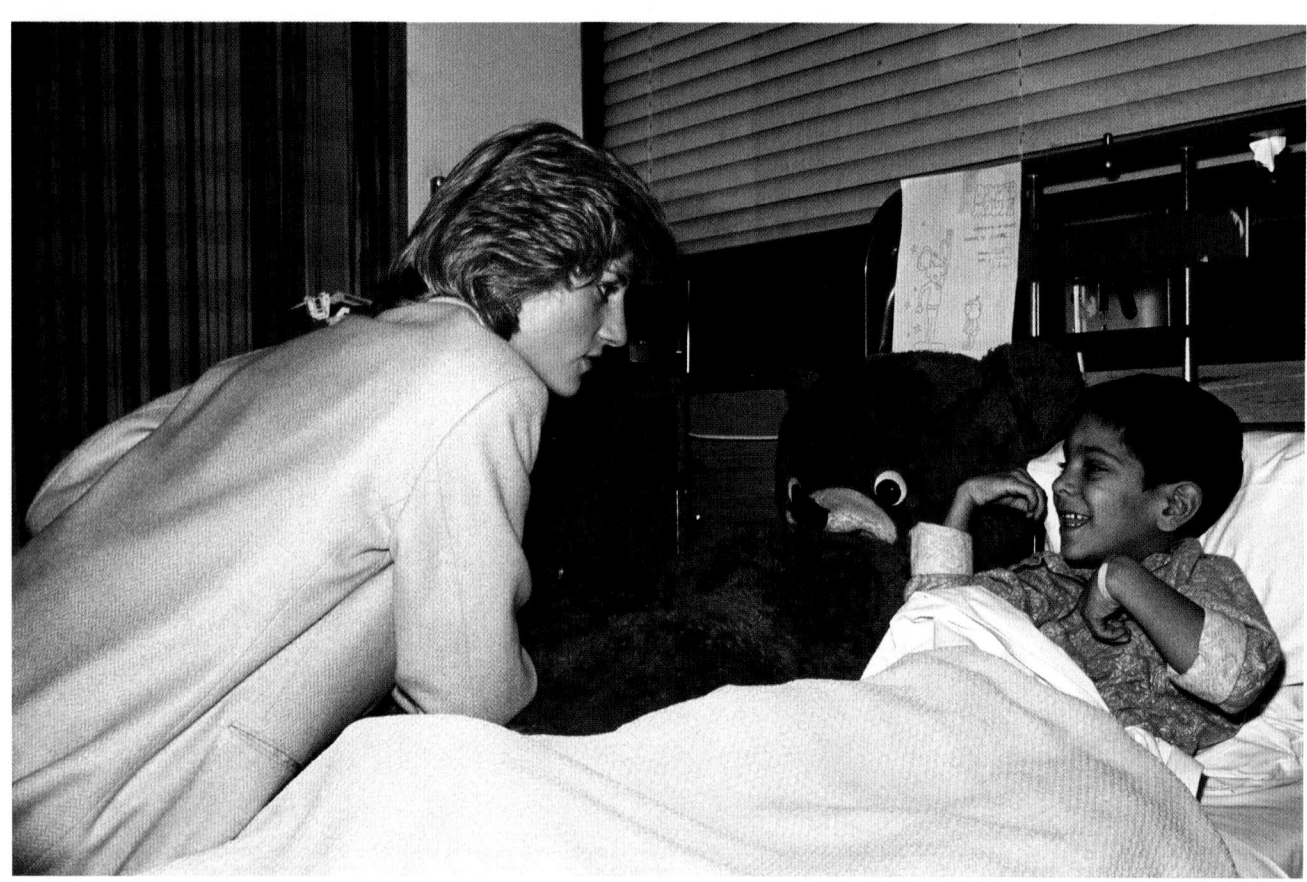

The Princess of Wales chats
to Rajan Parmar, of Palmers
Green, North London, in
bed with his teddy when the
Princess visited casualties of
the Harrods car bomb blast.
Rajan was recovering from a
leg injury and shock.
19th December, 1983

Eric Bristow celebrates with his winner's cheque and the trophy after his 7-1 final win over Dave Whitcombe in the Embassy World Professional Championship.

7th January, 1984

Debbie Harry, singer with the group Blondie who split up in this year. After an unsuccesful solo album 'Koo Koo', Harry took four years away from music to nurse her seriously ill partner and fellow Blondie band member, Chris Stein. Blondie reformed in 1998.

4th February, 1984

(L-R) Great Britain's Jayne Torvill and Christopher Dean wave to the crowd after receiving their gold medals for Ice Dance at the Sarajevo Winter Olympic Games.

14th February, 1984

The Thompson Twins arrive at Heathrow Airport from Germany after a television appearance for which they reportedly cancelled a sell-out concert the previous night at the Hammersmith Odeon. They are: Tom Bailey (L), Alannah Currie and Joe Leeway.

2nd March, 1984

A crowd of Yorkshire miners booed and barracked moderate NUM leaders when they arrived at the National Union of Miners HQ in Sheffield for the union's NEC meeting.
8th March, 1984

Boy George of Culture Club. The band was the first since The Beatles to achieve three US Top Ten hits from a debut album with their 'Kissing to be Clever' in 1982, and their 1983 release 'Karma Chameleon' was the best-selling single in the UK for that year, but 1984 was considered to see the beginning of the group's decline.

28th March, 1984

The Chair Jump at Aintree as eventual winner of the Grand National, 'Hallo Dandy' (28) ridden by Neale Doughty, goes clear of the mayhem behind, with 'Carl's Wager' losing his rider (amateur jockey Ronnie Beggan) and Graham Bradley rolls after falling from 'Ashley House'.
31st March, 1984

'Sea Goddess I', the most expensive cruise ship in the world, sails under Tower Bridge and out of London following her completion in the shipyards of Finland.
31st March, 1984

Pop phenomenon Madonna, in the year in which she achieved the first of a remarkable 17 consecutive Top Ten hits.
2nd April, 1984

Richard Cooke of Spurs
(L) gets into the action with
Norwich players Downs (R)
and Spearing during the
Canon League Division One
match at White Hart Lane,
London, which Spurs won
2-0.
5th May, 1984

Defending snooker champion Steve Davis (L) and his opponent Jimmy White with the trophy at the Crucible Theatre, Sheffield.
6th May, 1984

Four stars from the highly
popular television series
'Auf Wiedersehen Pet'
with news presenter Anne
Diamond, in London, prior to
the Pye Television Awards:
(back L-R) Gary Holton and
Christopher Fairbank; (front
L-R) Pat Roach and Kevin
Whately.
14th May, 1984

A group of Hells Angels moved into a £100,000 farmhouse on the Woburn Abbey estate with the blessing of Lord Tavistock. The Angels, members of the Nomads group, live rent-free in the cottage prompting claims that the Marquis had given in to threats.

14th May, 1984

Billy Connolly and Pamela
Stephenson with their
daughter Daisy after
arriving at Heathrow airport,
London, from St Lucia where
Connolly had been filming
'Water' with Michael Caine.
31st May, 1984

A picket calmly inspects a line of policemen outside the Orgreave Coking Plant near Rotherham. The 'Battle of Orgreave' saw the police use riot gear for the first time in the 1984-5 miners' strike when officers drafted in from 10 counties met 5,000 picketing miners.
4th June, 1984

Facing page: The Queen, US President Ronald Reagan and British Prime Minister Margaret Thatcher at Buckingham Palace when they attended a special banquet hosted by the Queen following the London Economic Summit.
9th June, 1984

Members of the Royal Family gather to watch the RAF flypast for the Queen's birthday. (L-R) The Prince of Wales, who is holding his son Prince William, the Duke of Kent, Princess Margaret, the Duchess of Gloucester, the Duke of Edinburgh, the Queen, Princess Michael of Kent, Zara Phillips (daughter of Princess Anne), the Princess of Wales and Lord Frederick Windsor (son of Princess Michael of Kent).
16th June, 1984

American tennis star John McEnroe holding up play in the final of the Stella Artois championship at Queen's Club by arguing with the umpire, who he called a 'moron'. McEnroe went on to beat his compatriot Leif Shiras 6-1, 3-6, 6-2.
17th June, 1984

Bob Dylan on stage at
Wembley.
8th July, 1984

Great Britain's Tessa
Sanderson celebrates with
her gold medal for the
Women's Javelin event at
the Los Angeles Olympic
Games.
6th August, 1984

Great Britain's Daley
Thompson in action in the
Shot Put event at the Los
Angeles Olympic Games.
8th August, 1984

Miners demonstrate with
placards outside the Trades
Union Congress conference
in Brighton.
3rd September, 1984

Television and radio
personality Terry Wogan
accepts 100 TV sets on
behalf of the NSPCC
from Phillips, marking the
production of the electronics
company's 100-millionth TV
set.
6th September, 1984

Policemen searching a youth near the Stock Exchange in London when a 'Stop The City' protest was expected to take place in the form of a demonstration by various groups.
27th September, 1984

Holly Johnson and Paul
Rutherford of Frankie Goes
To Hollywood outside the
Churchill Hotel trying out the
world's smallest compact
disc player, the Sony D-50.
9th October, 1984

Comedian Lenny Henry
and Dawn French on their
wedding day at St. Paul's
Church, Covent Garden,
London.
12th October, 1984

The Grand Hotel, Brighton, was severely damaged when an IRA bomb killed four people and injured 32 while the hotel was occupied by Margaret Thatcher and other prominent Tory Party members for the party conference.
12th October, 1984

The State Opening
of Parliament.
6th November, 1984

Comedian Ernie Wise
proudly displays one
of his famous short
fat hairy legs with
newsreader Angela Rippon.
9th November, 1984

Model Samantha Fox gives a preview in London of the London Mid-Season Show. One hundred and fifty fashion designers are showing their early Spring 1985 collections.

12th November, 1984

Nicholas Pierce, Managing
Director of Cellular One,
speaking to the USA using
the world's first truly portable
telephone, while cycling
through London.
22nd November, 1984

Annie Lennox and Dave
Stewart of The Eurythmics.
22nd November, 1984

Comedian Ernie Wise
and friends launching the
Racal-Vodafone computer-
controlled cellular radio
telephone service at St.
Katharine's Dock, London.
30th December, 1984

Bob Geldof arrives at
Heathrow Airport, where
he was greeted by his wife
Paula Yates, with their
daughter Fifi. Geldof had
just flown in from Ethiopa
and the Sudan, where he
witnessed the famine on
behalf of Band Aid.
14th January, 1985

Striking coal miner Ted Pickles from Denby Grange Colliery, near Wakefield, who has been busy entertaining miners' children as a circus clown. Mr Pickles from The Green, Ossett, has been swapping coal dust for greasepaint, part time, for 20 years.
22nd January, 1985

Dolman tops for models Joanna and Romilly in the Scots Fashion Show in London, at the Scottish Development Agency's Trade Development Centre.
4th February, 1985

Facing page: Terry Wogan (C) at the BBC TV centre in Shepherds Bush, London with American singer Tina Turner and pop star Elton John, two of the guests for his new chat show series.
18th February, 1985

The Queen with proprieter
Rupert Murdoch (L) at
the Times Newspaper
Building at Grays Inn Road,
London, to mark the paper's
bicentenary.
28th February, 1985

Midge Ure of Ultravox, who with Bob Geldof co-wrote the Band Aid single 'Do They Know It's Christmas?', spraying a message on a water tanker, bound for Ethiopia, at Gatwick Airport.
9th March, 1985

To the obvious delight of youngsters, the Prince of Wales tries his hand at breakdancing in a discotheque session. The Prince visited a Youth Meets Industry course for 300 unemployed young people at Middleton-on-Sea, organised by the Prince's Trust.
29th March, 1985

Facing page: A besuited punter tries his hand at dwarf tossing in Shakes Disco, Croydon.
26th April, 1985

George Cole, who plays
Arthur Daley in the television
series 'Minder'.
1st May, 1985

Spandau Ballet bassist
Martin Kemp and wife
Shirley at Heathrow Airport
in London after flying in from
New York.
11th May, 1985

Fifty six people died in a fire
at Bradford City FC's ground,
Valley Parade, during a
match with Lincoln City.
More than 250 supporters
were injured in the disaster.
11th May, 1985

Manchester United captain Bryan Robson lifts the FA Cup after his team beat Everton in the Final at Wembley.

18th May, 1985

Prime Minister Margaret Thatcher, watched by her husband Denis, lays a wreath among the hundreds of other floral tributes near the turnstile area of the Bradford City's football ground, where many of the 52 victims of the tragedy were found.
19th May, 1985

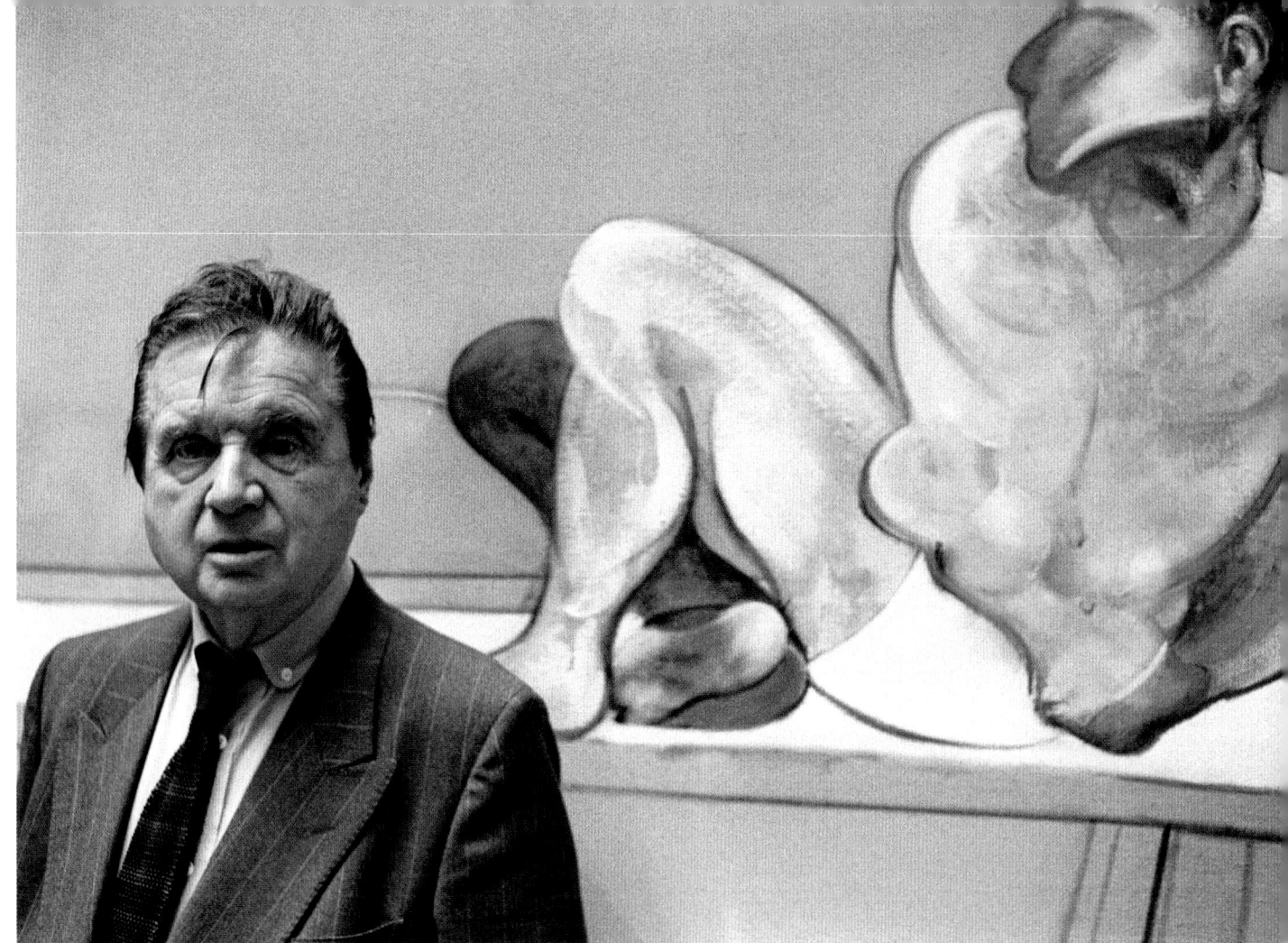

Artist Francis Bacon at the
Tate Gallery, London, during
a retrospective exhibition of
his work.
21st May, 1985

Diana, Princess of Wales,
and her youngest son Prince
Harry.
1st July, 1985

The Princess of Wales, the Prince of Wales and Sir Bob Geldof at Wembley for the Live Aid concert, organised by Geldof to raise millions of pounds for famine relief. Geldof's wife, Paula Yates, is on the right.

13th July, 1985

Tony Hadley, singer with
Spandau Ballet and one of
the voices featured on the
'Band Aid' single, performs
at the Live Aid concert.
13th July, 1985

Facing page: David Bowie
performs at the Live Aid
concert at Wembley.
13th July, 1985

72,000 people attended the Wembley Live Aid concert, while a further 90,000 attended JFK stadium, Philadelphia, for the 'global jukebox' that linked events in Britain, America and the Soviet Union. The concerts were broadcast live by satellite to an estimated audience of 1.5 billion.

13th July, 1985

Comedian Stanley Baxter during a break from filming, on location at Sprowston Hall Hotel, for a BBC One Christmas special. Mr Baxter returns to the BBC after a 14 year absence.
20th August, 1985

England's John Emburey (L), Mike Gatting (second L), Paul Downton (fifth L), Phil Edmonds (fourth R), David Gower (third R), Ian Botham (second R) and Allan Lamb (R) appeal for the wicket of Australia's Wayne Phillips (fourth L) following Gower's catch of a ball which deflected off Lamb's boot. The Ashes Fifth Test at Edgebaston.
20th August, 1985

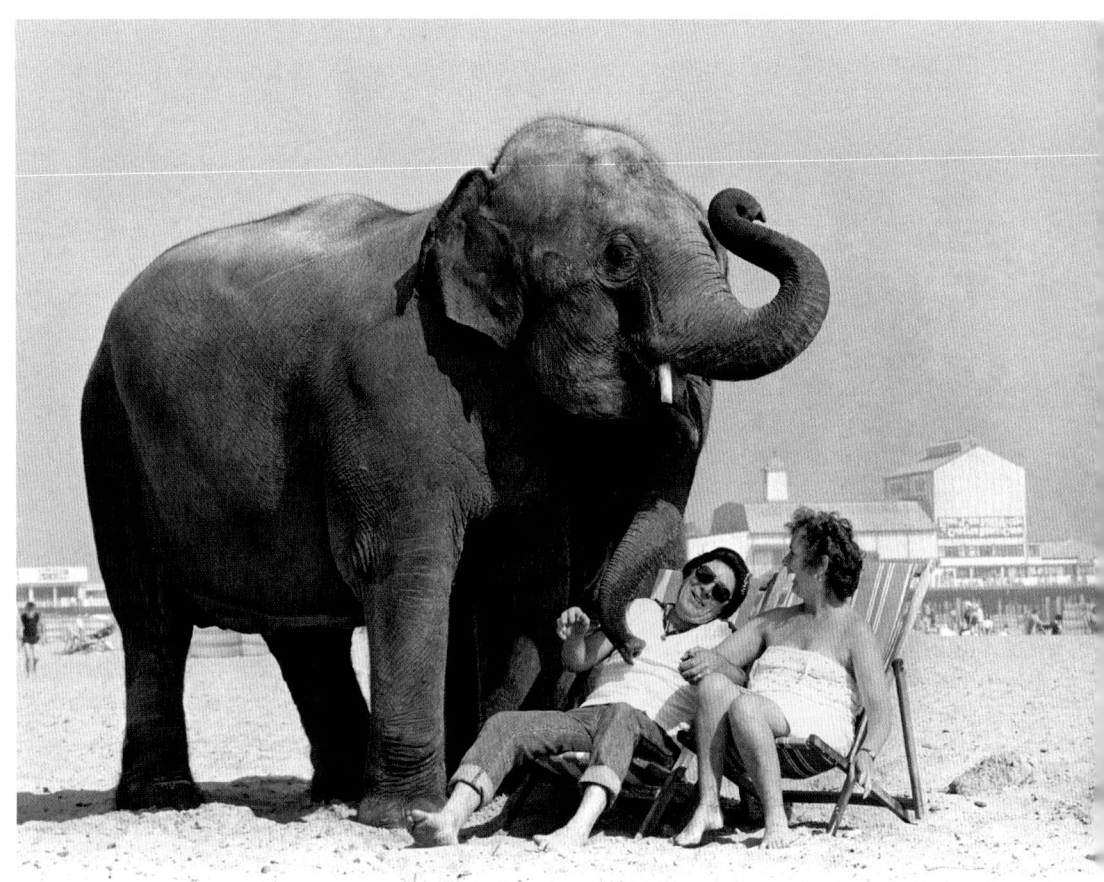

Circus elephants make friends with holidaymakers Graham and Janet Stead, of Stapleford, Notts, on the beach at Great Yarmouth.
2nd September, 1985

The Princess of Wales on board the Forties Charlie platform on a visit to the North Sea Forties oil field.
3rd September, 1985

The European team celebrate with the Ryder Cup: (back row L-R) Jose Rivero, Bernhard Langer, Nick Faldo, Sam Torrance, captain Tony Jacklin, Sandy Lyle, Paul Way, Ken Brown and Seve Ballesteros; (front row L-R) Howard Clark, Ian Woosnam, Jose-Maria Canizares and Manuel Pinero.
15th September, 1985

One person was killed,
50 injured and over 200
arrested during riots in
Brixton, South London, after
police shot Cherry Groce,
the mother of a robbery
suspect, in her bed when
they raided her house in the
early hours. Mrs Groce was
crippled by the shooting and
spent two years in hospital.
28th September, 1985

Su Pollard in her signature
role of holiday camp chalet
maid Peggy, in BBC-TV's
'Hi-De-Hi'.
1st October, 1985

Anti-Thatcher graffiti left by
Protestant protestors in the
shadow of the Harland and
Wolff shipyard in Belfast
following the signing of the
Anglo-Irish Agreement,
which gave the Irish
Republic a consultative role
in Northern Ireland.
18th November, 1985

Prime Minister Margaret Thatcher is joined by the Queen and five former PMs at 10 Downing Street, London, on the 250th anniversary of the residence becoming the London home of British Prime Ministers: (L-R) James Callaghan, Lord Home, Mrs Thatcher, Lord Stockton, the Queen, Lord Wilson and Edward Heath.
4th December, 1985

Prime Minister Margaret
Thatcher and French
President Francois Mitterand
at Canterbury Cathedral for
the signing of the Channel
Fixed Link Treaty, clearing
the way for the construction
of the Channel Tunnel.
13th February, 1986

Michael Barrymore and
Anneka Rice, joint winners
of the 1986 Rear of the Year
award.
23rd February, 1986

England's Gary Rees (R) feeds his backs, watched by teammates Dean Richards (third L), Nigel Melville (second L) and Wade Dooley (L) in the Five Nations Championship – England v Ireland.

1st March, 1986

Lead singer of The Who, Roger Daltrey, pulling a punch on Eddie Large with the help of Syd Little. The last in the series of 'The Little and Large Show' was to be aired on April 5th.
3rd March, 1986

Tights from the 'Fantasy' range modelled by Katie at the Ritz Hotel.
6th March, 1986

Model Linda Lusardi wears a
tropical print cotton sundress
from the Spring and Summer
Collection of Richards, at the
Tropicana Show.
11th March, 1986

Comedienne Victoria
Wood, with her BAFTA
Award for The Best Light
Entertainment Performance
for 'Victoria Wood as Seen
on TV'.
17th March, 1986

Gary Lineker of Everton, chosen as Player of the Year by his fellow footballers, and Everton manager Howard Kendall (R) with the trophy at Goodison Park.

23rd March, 1986

Cockney pop stars Chas 'n' Dave (C) with the 'Match Room Mob' on the release of their single 'Snooker Loopy', appropriately enough planned for April the First. The 'Mob' are snooker players (L-R) Willie Thorne, Tony Meo, Terry Griffiths, Dennis Taylor and Steve Davis.

26th March, 1986

One person died and the upper floors of the south wing of historic Hampton Court Palace were devastated by fire. Many priceless art treasures were destroyed or damaged.
31st March, 1986

The Prince Wales playing pool on a visit to see young unemployed people on a Work, Sport and Leisure course at a holiday camp in Caister-on-Sea, Norfolk.
25th April, 1986

Deputy Assistant
Commissioner Wyn Jones
displays some of the
missiles thrown at police
during the previous night's
picket line violence at the
News International plant at
Wapping, East London.
4th May, 1986

Presenters of BBC
Television's 'Tomorrow's
World': (L-R) James Burke,
Judith Hann, Raymond
Baxter, Maggie Philbin,
Peter Macann and Howard
Stableford. The show
attracted audiences of 10
million.
6th May, 1986

Liverpool player-manager Kenny Dalglish (second L) shows off the League Championship trophy as teammate Mark Lawrenson (third L) displays the FA Cup during the team's celebratory open-topped bus journey through the city, the day after they completed the Double.
11th May, 1986

Virgin tycoon Richard Branson was celebrating after he smashed the world record for the fastest crossing of the Atlantic in his powerboat 'Virgin Challenger II'. He is pictured at the boat's launch at Lowestoft.

14th May, 1986

England's John Barnes (L)
and Gary Lineker training
hard for the World Cup in
Mexico.
1st June, 1986

TV personality Kenny Everett with the new line up of dance group Hot Gossip. The dancers will be appearing in the new series of 'The Kenny Everett Television Show' on BBC 1.

18th June, 1986

Argentina's Diego Maradona (R) flies past England goalkeeper Peter Shilton (L) after using his fist to score the opening goal – the infamous 'Hand of God' goal – in the quarter-final of the Mexico World Cup.
22nd June, 1986

Britain's Nigel Mansell
(foreground) in action during
the British Grand Prix at
Silverstone.
14th July, 1986

The sweat flies when Frank Bruno (R) and the WBA World Heavyweight Champion Tim Witherspoon both land punches simultaneously during their clash. Witherspoon, of Philadelphia, USA, retained his title after the referee stopped the fight in the 11th round.

20th July, 1986

Prince Andrew kisses his
bride Sarah Ferguson on
the balcony of Buckingham
Palace on their wedding day.
23rd July, 1986

Cinema manager Bill Heine
hired a crane to lower a
25 foot glass-fibre shark,
sculpted by John Buckley,
onto the roof of his house
in Headington, Oxfordshire,
to commemorate the
anniversary of the Nagasaki
atom bomb.
10th August, 1986

HMS 'Brazan' is escorted
by a flotilla of small boats
into Malta's Grand Harbour
at Valletta, where it was
greeted with an emotional
welcome from the islanders,
seven years after the Royal
Navy was forced to leave its
shores.
16th August, 1986

Welsh stunt motorcyclist Chris Bromham practising for his world record attempt at the Royal Victoria Docks, London, later that month. This resulted in his second entry into the Guinness Book of Records, under Ramp Jumping, for the distance of 241 feet.

17th August, 1986

You can park them anywhere. A Mini crashed off the top storey of a car park, landing on its big brother, the Maxi.
4th September, 1986

Facing page: Comedian Benny Hill with his 'Hill's Angels': (top L-R) Selina Caston, Lorraine Doyle, Sue Upton and Natalie Rolls; (bottom L-R) Zoe Bryant and Liz Jobling.
1st September, 1986

Santa Claus hands out Christmas cards to two punk rockers in Trafalgar Square, London at the launch of a special offer by the National Dairy Council and breakfast cereal giant Kelloggs to help raise £250,000 for children's charities.
18th September, 1986

Prime Minister Margaret
Thatcher addresses
the Commonwealth
Parliamentary Conference,
watched by the Queen
as the Duke of Edinburgh
listens.
25th September, 1986

'Spitting Image' puppets
of Prime Minister Margaret
Thatcher, US President
Ronald Reagan and
Japanese Prime Minister
Yasuhiro Nakasone during
filming aboard HMS 'Belfast'.
10th October, 1986

Dealing on the new high technology computer systems begins on the floor of the London Stock Exchange as the City's 'Big Bang' shake-up takes off.
27th October, 1986

Dennis Taylor takes to
the table in the Benson &
Hedges Masters Snooker
Tournament at Wembley,
London.
1st February, 1987

Past and present members of the cast of children's TV series 'Grange Hill' celebrate the programme's 10th anniversary at the BBC's Elstree Centre in Borehamwood: (L-R) Susan Tully, John McMahon, Mark Baxter, Alison Bettles and Todd Carty.

3rd February, 1987

Paddington Bear flanked
by can-can dancers Sarah
Dangerfield and Sara Bracci
at London's Paddington
Station during the launch of
the Eurotunnel Exhibition
Train.
2nd March, 1987

Rescue vessels surround the stricken Herald of Free Enterprise outside Zeebrugge, after the car ferry left port with its bow doors open. 193 people died in the disaster, which took place just 100 yards from the shore in near freezing water. A rescue operation by the Belgian Navy saved many lives.

6th March, 1987

The Duchess of York, after
becoming the first female
member of the Royal family
to gain a private pilot's
licence, went on to the
flight deck of a Concorde
supersonic jet during a visit
to Heathrow Airport.
11th March, 1987

Novelist Kingsley Amis, who won the prestigious Booker Prize with his book 'The Old Devils'.
14th March, 1987

World Heavyweight
Champion Mike Tyson
at Wembley Stadium to
promote his upcoming fight
against Frank Bruno.
15th March, 1987

David Bowie at a London
press conference to promote
his forthcoming world tour
for the Aids Campaign.
20th March, 1987

The 'Herald of Free
Enterprise' is hauled almost
upright in a winching
operation which took more
than eight hours by Dutch
salvage company Smit Tak.
7th April, 1987

(L-R) Fuji Yamada, Mitzi Mueller, Gorgeous George, Kendo Nagasaki, 'Mighty' John Quinn and Klondyke Kate, all taking part in a six bout wrestling programme at the Royal Albert Hall in London.
9th April, 1987

Comedy duo Tommy Cannon (R) and Bobby Ball, 'Cannon and Ball' with model Erica Preston outside the London Palladium, where they will be appearing in 'Babes in the Wood' next Christmas.
9th April, 1987

Facing page: The Duchess of York prepares for an hour-long flight over the Lincolnshire countryside in a Red Arrows Bulldog trainer aircraft during her visit to the team's base at RAF Scampton.
7th May, 1987

Labour leader Neil Kinnock bowling, watched by his wife Glenys, at the Stevenage Leisure Centre during campaigning for the General Election.
6th June, 1987

Facing page: The Princess of Wales (R) and the Duchess of York (L), forming a fashionable trio of hats and shoulders with a third visitor in the Royal Enclosure at Royal Ascot.
16th June, 1987

'Opportunity Knocks' presenter Bob Monkhouse gives a lift to nine year old singer Toni Warne, from Ipswich, outside the London Palladium theatre. Toni was the youngest ever three-times winner, and continues to sing professionally 20 years later.

19th June, 1987

U2 singer and campaigner Bono, born Paul Hewson. A stage-stealing performance at Live Aid and 1987's album 'The Joshua Tree' catapulted U2 to international star status, giving Bono a platform for his campaigns, including debt relief for developing countries, world poverty and Aids.
28th June, 1987

Nigel Mansell sits on the wheel of his car as he poses for pictures with the Williams Honda Formula One team.
11th July, 1987

The Queen Mother enjoys a pint of bitter which she pulled herself, during a visit to The Queen's Head pub in Stepney in London's East End.

16th July, 1987

Nick Faldo celebrates
winning the 116th British
Open Golf Championship at
Muirfield.
17th July, 1987

Captains Diego Maradona (L) and Brian Robson shake hands before the football match between the Football League side and the Rest of the World at Wembley.
8th August, 1987

The Prince of Wales negotiating a wire bridge during a trek in the foothills of Ben Nevis with the Lochaber Mountain Rescue Team.
18th August, 1987

American singer Madonna during her first London concert, at Wembley Stadium.
18th August, 1987

Children's television presenters Phillip Schofield and Sarah Greene on the 'hot line' in London, as they prepare to host BBC 1's new Saturday morning programme 'Going Live', which features phone-in involvement from viewers at home.

21st September, 1987

A giant envelope containing a letter calling for Britain to support a nuclear bomb test ban treaty is delivered to the Prime Minister: (L-R) Emma Thompson, Anna Carteret, Robbie Coltrane, Sir Rudolf Peierls (designer of the first atom bomb) and Bill Oddie.
1st October, 1987

Across the southern parts of England trees were uprooted and buildings damaged in what came to be known as the Great Storm. Frixos Pallas and his family had a lucky escape in the early hours of the morning when this tree demolished his home in Caversham, Reading.

16th October, 1987

Virtuoso beer mat flipper
Dean Gould, of Suffolk,
breaks his own world record
by catching 93 mats in
London's Covent Garden
Piazza. Mr Gould was
taking part in the launch
of the 1988 edition of 'The
Guinness Book of Records'.
19th October, 1987

Rock star Phil Collins and actress Julie Walters eat fish and chips in South London on the first day's shoot of the film 'Buster', which tells the story of Great Train Robber, Buster Edwards.

25th October, 1987

The Democratic Unionist
Party leader, the Reverend
Ian Paisley.
14th November, 1987

Elton John during a dress rehearsal for the Royal Gala Performance in aid of the Prince's Trust at the London Palladium.
4th December, 1987

Jill Morrell lights a candle for her boyfriend, kidnapped television reporter John McCarthy, during a vigil at St Bride's Church in Fleet Street, London.
31st December, 1987

Five ships from NATO's
multi-national minehunting
squadron, the Standing
Naval Force Channel
(SNFC), pass under Tower
Bridge on the River Thames
to berth alongside HMS
'Belfast' (R) at the start of a
three-day visit to London.
29th January, 1988

Actors Michael Caine and Ben Kingsley find some Comic Relief on the set of a new Sherlock Holmes film, 'Sherlock and Me', at Pinewood Studios with a pair of now-ubiquitous red noses in time for Red Nose Day.

3rd February, 1988

Eddie 'The Eagle' Edwards was working as a plasterer when he qualified, as the sole British applicant, for the 1988 Winter Olympics ski-jumping competition. Although the media liked to represent him solely as a comedy figure, he had previously represented Great Britain at the 1987 World Championships and was ranked 55th in the world.
16th February, 1988

TUC General Secretary Norman Willis (centre, front), with union leaders Clive Jenkins (ASTMS, right of Willis), Rodney Bickerstaffe (NUPE, taller man left of Willis) and nurses assemble on Victoria Embankment to lead a march in protest at Government polices towards the National Health Service.
5th March, 1988

Junior health minister
Edwina Currie shows how
to dump the smoking habit
as she launches the UK's
first smoke-free betting
shop, owned by Ladbrokes,
in London's West End on
National No Smoking Day.
9th March, 1988

Dame Edna Everage (alias Barry Humphries) races into the fashion stakes in Chelsea, after being fitted out with a new look by Royal designers David and Elizabeth Emanuel. Dame Edna had the outfit made for 'her' charity appearance in the gala 'Sunday with Sondheim'.
25th March, 1988

Displaying a model of the proposed Canary Wharf in London's Docklands, at the Queen Elizabeth II Conference Centre in London are (L-R) Paul Reichmann of Olympia & York, the scheme's developers, Sir Roy Strong, advisor on open spaces to the developers and Michael Dennis, head of the Canary Wharf project.
29th March, 1988

George Michael performing in concert. Michael released his first solo album, 'Faith', in October 1987: it was to achieve great success, particularly in the USA where it became 1988's best-selling album overall.
1st April, 1988

The Lady of Calcutta meets the Iron Lady: Mother Teresa and Prime Minister Margaret Thatcher at 10 Downing Street, London, after Mother Teresa had pledged to ask for help in setting up a hostel for London's homeless.
13th April, 1988

Jacqueline goes for a medieval look in London as she models one of the outfits from Laura Ashley's Autumn/ Winter 1988 Collection.
20th April, 1988

Wimbledon celebrate with
the FA Cup after beating
Liverpool 1-0.
14th May, 1988

The **1980s** Britain in Pictures

Steffi Graf lifts the Ladies' Singles trophy after her three-set victory over Martina Navratilova at Wimbledon.
3rd July, 1988

Fans of Nigel Mansell
display a banner at
Silverstone.
10th July, 1988

Facing page: The Piper
Alpha oil rig burns off the
coast of Aberdeen in the
North Sea. 167 people died
of around 225 workers on
the rig, in the world's worst
offshore oil disaster.
8th July, 1988

Nigel Mansell throws his
cap into a throng of fans
after finishing second in the
British Grand Prix.
10th July, 1988

American superstar Michael Jackson rocks Wembley Stadium in London, as he kicks off the British leg of a sell-out world tour.
14th July, 1988

Eastenders' actors Pam
St Clement and Mike Reid
share a pint at the Televison
Centre in London, when the
new landlady and landlord
of the Queen Vic pub helped
launch BBC1's £62 million
lineup of programmes.
16th August, 1988

Customers enjoying a quiet lunchtime drink in Farnborough look skywards as a giant aircraft, the Soviet AN-124 transport plane – the biggest aircraft in the world – flies in for the Farnborough Air Show.
30th August, 1988

LEADING BRITAIN
INTO THE 1990s

Facing page: Freddie
Mercury and Monserrat
Caballe perform their hit
song 'Barcelona' during an
outdoor concert held on
the slopes of Barcelona's
Montjuich park, to celebrate
the arrival of the Olympic
flag from Seoul.
9th October, 1988

Margaret Thatcher's
closing speech is projected
onto a TV monitor at
the Conservative Party
Conference, Brighton.
14th October, 1988

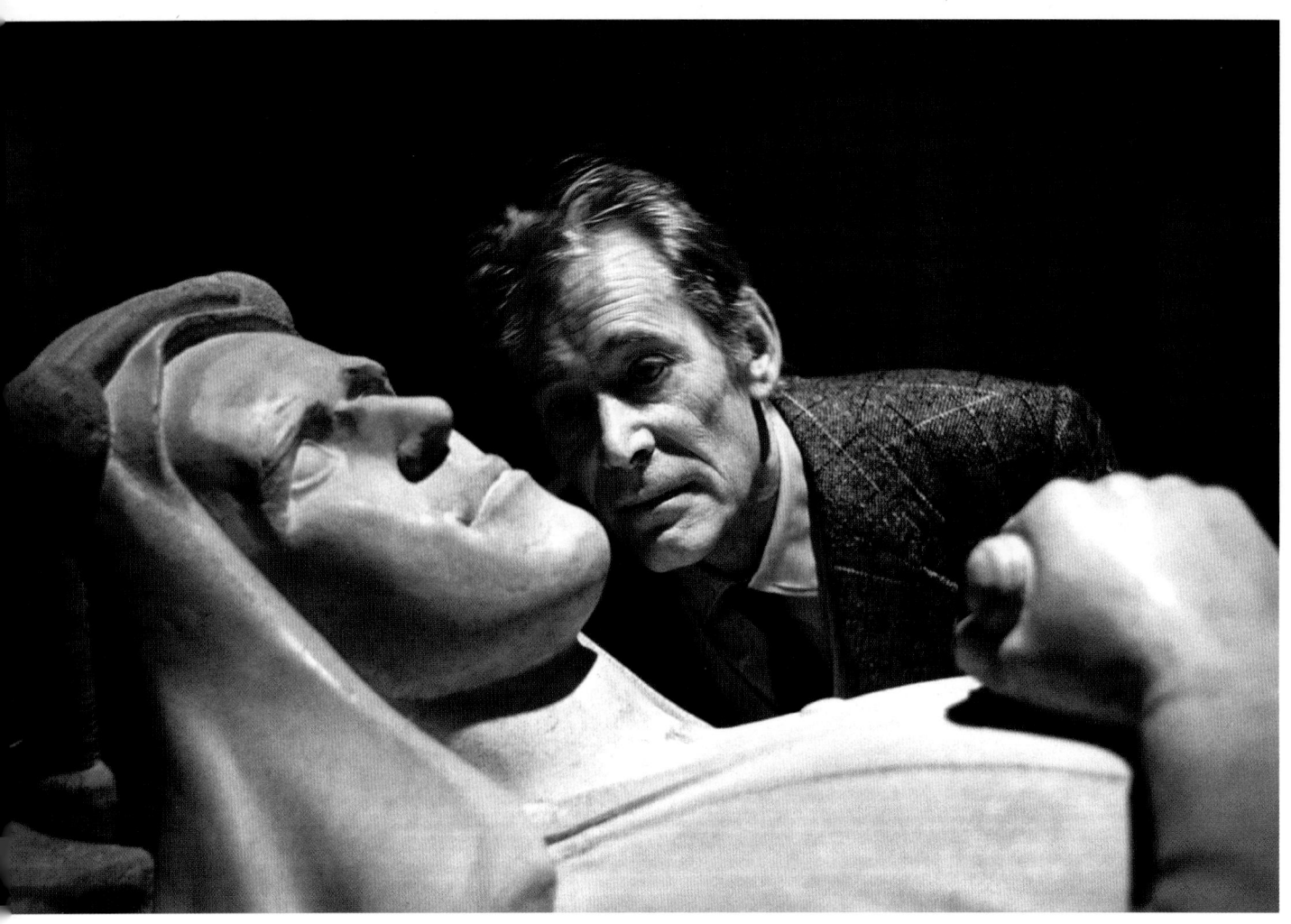

Actor Peter O'Toole views a
cement cast of Eric Kennington's
portrait of T E Lawrence at
the National Portrait Gallery
in London, before the opening
of an exhibition to mark the
centenary of his birth in 1888.
8th December, 1988

One of Britain's worst rail disasters occured just outside Clapham Junction railway station. 35 people died when a London-bound commuter train ploughed into a stationary train.
12th December, 1988

The Duke and Duchess of York with their daughter, 18 week old Princess Beatrice, leaving the Chapel Royal at St. James' Palace in London after her christening.
20th December, 1988

The wrecked nose section
of the Pan-Am Boeing 747
lies in a Scottish field at
Lockerbie, near Dumfries,
after the plane, which had
been flying from Frankfurt to
New York, was blown apart
by a terrorist bomb.
22nd December, 1988

The tail section of the
wrecked British Midlands
Boeing 737 flying from
Heathrow to Belfast, which
plunged into an embankment
on the M1 motorway in
Leicestershire. 46 people
were killed.
9th January, 1989

Television presenter Frank
Bough fronting a special
exhibition stand at Waterloo
Station in London where
commuters were given a
glimpse of programmes
on offer from SKY TV, the
satellite broadcasting station.
6th February, 1989

Salman Rushdie, author
of the controversial 'The
Satanic Verses', which
resulted in the 1989 fatwa
issued by Ayatollah Ruhollah
Khomeini, ordering Muslims
to kill him.
14th February, 1989

The Duchess of York greets Dustin Hoffman and Tom Cruise at London's Empire Leicester Square, for the charity movie premiere of the film 'Rainman' in aid of MIND, the National Association for Mental Health.
22nd February, 1989

Actor John Pertwee and
a colleague promoting a
stage production of the
long-running BBC Television
series 'Dr Who', opening at
the Wimbledon Theatre in
London with Pertwee in the
title role.
23rd February, 1989

Kylie Minogue and Jason
Donovan don red noses for
Comic Relief, raising money
for Africa and disadvantaged
people in Britain.
7th March, 1989

'Desert Orchid', Simon Sherwood up, races to a famous victory in the Cheltenham Gold Cup. The race was a mile longer than the horse's believed preference, and rain and snow made the going heavier than he liked. Racing Post readers voted it the best horse race ever.
16th March, 1989

Pop group Duran Duran take a break from rehearsals at the London Arena at Limeharbour in London's Docklands, before starting a nationwide tour in Newcastle: (L-R) Nick Rhodes, Simon Le Bon, Sterling Campbell, Warren Cuccurullo and John Taylor.
13th April, 1989

Thousands gathered around
a pitch full of flowers at
Anfield Stadium, for the
Ceremony of Remembrance
for those who died in the
tragic Hillsborough disaster a
week earlier.
22nd April, 1989

Protesting prisoners at
Risley Remand Centre,
Cheshire, line up on the roof
before ending their three-day
occupation of D Wing.
3rd May, 1989

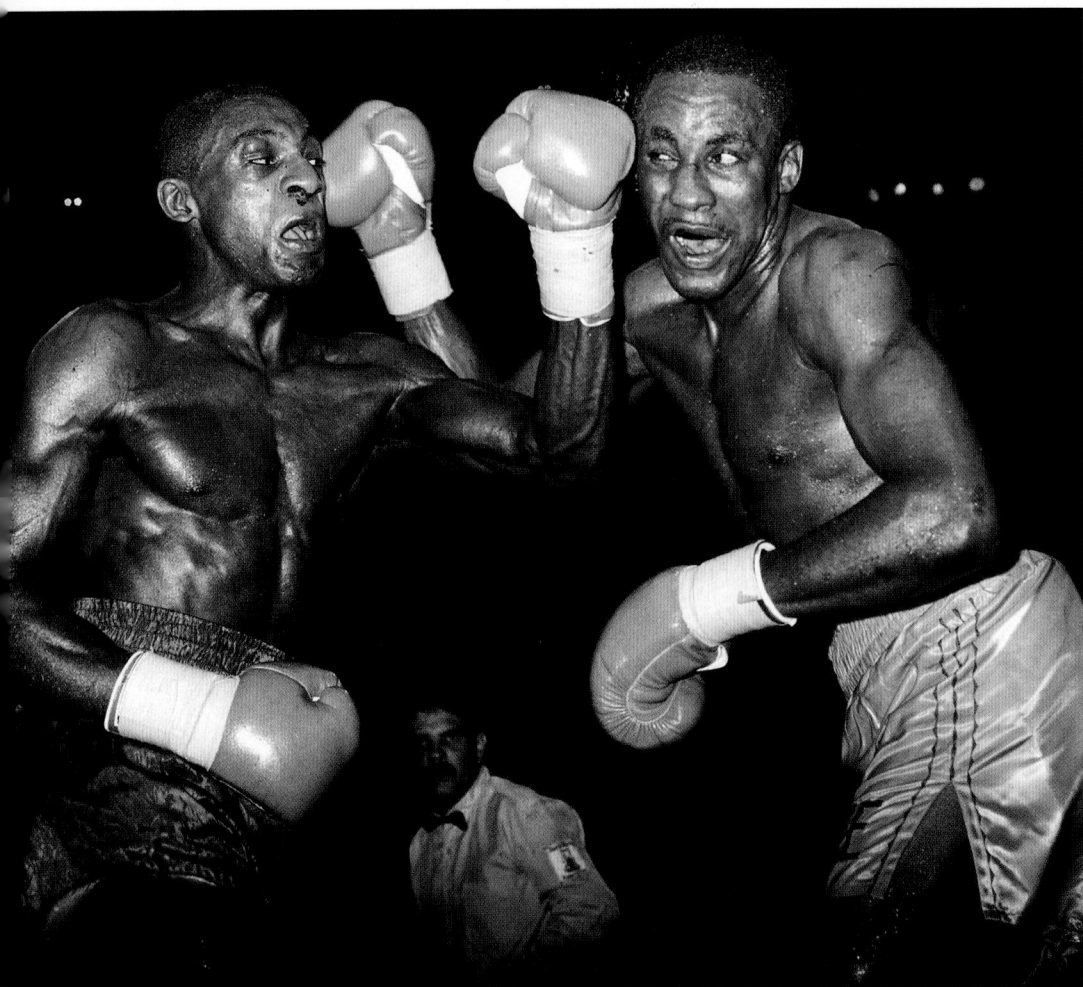

Sheffield's Herol Graham (L) and New York's Mike McCallum feel each other's punching power during the vacant WBA World Middleweight Championship fight at the Royal Albert Hall, London. McCallum beat Graham on a split points decision.

10th May, 1989

Stepping out from an East London Undergound station after their 'passing out parade' are four members of London's first New York style Guardian Angels Chapter: (L-R) Ian Carter, Venca Hughes, American founder Curtis Sliwa, Nicky Howard and Darren Champness.

14th May, 1989

John Barnes, Liverpool, in
the FA Cup Final – Liverpool
v Everton.
20th May, 1989

Radio personality Tony
Blackburn in a Capital Radio
studio in Euston, London
celebrating 25 years as a
radio disc jockey.
23rd July, 1989

Musician and famine fund-raiser Bob Geldof and his wife, television presenter Paula Yates.
7th September, 1989

Facing page: Christy O'Connor celebrates after his putt on the eighteenth hole won the Ryder Cup for Europe.
24th September, 1989

The Guildford Four were
cleared of all charges and
released after 14 years
in prison having been
wrongfully convicted of
IRA bombings on the UK
mainland. Gerard Conlon,
one of the Guildford Four,
outside the Old Bailey after
his release.
19th October, 1989

The control room for monitoring television cameras in the Commons. Television viewers will be able to watch the State Opening of Parliament on November 21, the day the new facility commences.

2nd November, 1989

The Princess of Wales
meets Joan Collins at a
Gala Dinner in aid of the
AIDS Crisis Trust, held at
Cliveden House, Berkshire.
The guests include Barry
Humphries (L) and Marie
Helvin (second R).
22nd November, 1989

Virgin tycoon Richard
Branson and his co-pilot,
Swedish aero-engineer
Per Lindstrand, after their
planned balloon crossing of
the Pacific from Miyakonjo,
Japan, was aborted.
27th November, 1989

The Publishers gratefully acknowledge PA Photos, from whose extensive archive the photographs in this book have been selected. Personal copies of the photographs in this book, and many others, may be ordered online at www.prints.paphotos.com

For more information, please contact:

Ammonite Press

AE Publications Ltd. 166 High Street, Lewes, East Sussex, BN7 1XU, United Kingdom
Tel: 01273 488005 Fax: 01273 402866
www.ae-publications.com